IN ANCIENT GREECE

PHILIP
SAUVAIN

ILLUSTRATIONS BY
GRAHAM
HUMPHREYS

new
DISCOVERY
B·O·O·K·S
New York

Maxwell Macmillan Canada
Toronto

Maxwell Macmillan International
New York • Oxford • Singapore • Sydney

First American publication 1992 by New Discovery Books, Macmillan
Publishing Company, 866 Third Avenue, New York, NY 10022
Maxwell Macmillan Canada Inc., 1200 Eglinton Avenue East, Suite 200,
Don Mills, Ontario M3C 3N1

Macmillan Publishing Company is part of the Maxwell Communication
Group of Companies

First published in Great Britain by Zoe Books Limited, 15 Worthy Lane,
Winchester, Hampshire SO23 7AB

A ZOË BOOK

Devised and produced by
Zoe Books Limited
15 Worthy Lane
Winchester
Hampshire SO23 7AB
England

Printed in Belgium

10 9 8 7 6 5 4 3 2 1

Library of Congress Cataloging-in-Publication Data

Sauvain, Philip Arthur.
   Over 2,000 years ago: in ancient Greece/by Philip Arthur Sauvain.
   p. cm. — (History detectives)
   Includes index.
   Summary: Describes what life was life in ancient Greece, discussing
such aspects as meals, the army, theater, and sports.
   ISBN 0-02-781082-8
   1. Greece — Social life and customs — Juvenile literature.
[1. Greece — Civilization — To 146 B.C.] I. Title. II. Series.
DF78.S2   1992
938 — dc20   91-40072

Design: Pardoe Blacker
Picture research: Sarah Staples
Illustrations: G. Humphreys

Photographic acknowledgments

The publishers wish to acknowledge, with thanks, the following
photographic sources:

7, 15t Ronald Sheridan/Ancient Art and Architecture Collection; 15b
Michael Holford; 18 Ashmolean Museum Library; 19 Ronald
Sheridan/Ancient Art and Architecture Collection; 23 Michael Holford

Contents

THE ACROPOLIS

People have lived in the country now called Greece for more than 40,000 years. At first they hunted for food and gathered wild fruits. Later they became farmers. About 6,500 years ago people found out how to mix the metals tin and copper to make another metal called bronze. They used this new metal to make tools and weapons.

With better tools, farmers could produce more food. Some of the extra, or surplus, food was exchanged for other goods, and trading began. Trade made people richer, so the population grew and cities like Athens were built. It was the beginning of the Greek civilization.

This picture shows a religious procession more than 2,400 years ago. The people of the city of Athens are climbing the steep hill called the Acropolis, which means "high city." They are going to the temple called the Parthenon, at the top of the hill.

The Acropolis was the center of Athens 3,000 years ago. It was protected by being built on a huge rock and by its high walls. As the city grew in size, homes and public buildings were also built in the valley below.

This huge statue of the goddess Athena stood inside the Parthenon. It was made of gold and ivory, and was more than 40 feet (12 meters) high. Nothing is left today, but a description by a Greek writer called Pausanias and pictures on coins tell us what it looked like.

Greek worshipers brought gifts to offer to Athena. They also killed animals and offered them to the goddess.

Gods and goddesses

Stories, poems, and plays by Greek writers such as Homer tell us a great deal about the Greeks. Homer's stories say that the people of Greece thought that the god Zeus reigned over the other gods and goddesses. The Greeks thought the gods and goddesses lived on the cloud-covered top of Mount Olympus in northern Greece. Each god or goddess looked after a different part of the Greeks' daily life. Sailors worshiped Poseidon, the god of the sea. Farmers prayed to Dionysus, god of wine. The Greeks also admired the heroines and heroes in the stories or legends about Greek history, such as Jason and the Golden Fleece, or Perseus and Medusa.

Athena, the daughter of Zeus, was the goddess of wisdom and war. She was one of the most important of the gods and goddesses. The Greeks believed that Athena protected the people of the towns and cities. This is why she was usually shown in a helmet and armor. Her special sign or symbol was an owl. The Athenians named their city Athens after her, and they built the Parthenon on the Acropolis as her temple.

We know about ancient Greece because the people left behind clues, or evidence, about their lives. Some clues are in writing or in pictures. Paintings on vases show scenes from daily life. Statues show what people looked like. Other clues, such as tools, coins, weapons, and jewelry, have been found by archaeologists and are now in museums. We can also visit the ruins of the Acropolis and some of the other buildings the Greeks used.

The Parthenon is the best-known building on the Acropolis, but other temples were built there as well. The Erechtheum was the temple of Erectheus, who was one of the founders of Athens, according to legend. Near the temples stood a huge statue of Athena. Her helmet reflected the sun, and could be seen far out at sea as ships sailed toward the city's port at Piraeus.

The Athenians brought wine, oil, and other gifts to offer to Athena so that she would protect them. Every four years they held a festival called the Panathenaea to honor Athena. The people walked in a procession up to the Acropolis. They entered the temple area through a huge gateway called the Propylaea. The festival lasted for six days.

This is the Parthenon today. How is it different from the picture on the previous page? The Athenian architect Ictinus began work on the Parthenon in 447 B.C., helped by a builder called Callicrates and the sculptor Phidias. They completed it in 438 B.C.

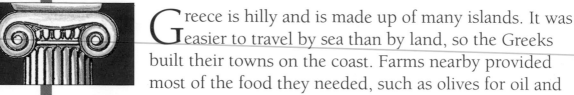

THE GREEK CITIES

Greece is hilly and is made up of many islands. It was easier to travel by sea than by land, so the Greeks built their towns on the coast. Farms nearby provided most of the food they needed, such as olives for oil and grapes to make wine. Greek merchants used ships to carry goods such as pottery, honey, or silver, which they traded for corn and other goods. Greek cities charged the traders a fee, or customs duty, on the goods, so many cities became rich. Athens was the chief trading center.

Each city governed itself and the area surrounding it. We call this a city-state. We know most about the city-state of Athens. About 2,500 years ago Athens was a democracy, which means that the state was governed by the people.

All the male adult citizens of Athens could speak and vote at meetings of the Assembly. The speaker stood on a stone step, the podium, to address the crowd. Greek women were not allowed to take part in government. Neither women nor slaves could speak or vote at the Assembly. They did not even attend the meetings.

Ancient Greece was a man's world. The men of Athens did most of the shopping. They went every day to the large square in the city center. The square was called the agora. It was the place where people heard all the news and the gossip. There they met friends and argued about politics.

9

The agora

The agora of a Greek city was surrounded by the main buildings of the city. There were law courts, government buildings, the army headquarters, and the mint, where coins were made. The agora was also the main market. Traders on market stalls sold pots, metal goods, bread, fish, cloth, herbs, fruit, and many other goods. The agora was always crowded with shoppers and merchants. Nearby were the workshops of many of the craftspeople of the city. These included shoemakers, weavers, metalworkers, potters, and carpenters. Merchants sold goods from other states or countries in shops in the agora.

Poorer women had to collect their own water from the public fountains. They met friends at the well, and heard the latest news.

Slaves working at a forge. As many as one person in every three was a slave in Athens. Slaves were usually well treated and were often paid a wage. Some slaves were able to buy their freedom.

Most people earned their living by selling or making goods. Small workshops where one or two free men and a few slaves worked were built next to people's homes. There were no workplaces such as factories. Only in the mines were there lots of people at work together. At Laurium silver mine there were about 20,000 slaves at work.

Women worked at home, where they organized all the work of the household. They also spun and wove cloth on an upright loom. They made all the cloth for clothes and furnishings for the household.

In Athens, married women from wealthy families did not often go out, except on family visits or for religious festivals. If they did go to the agora, they always took a slave with them. In poorer families the women had to do more housework and shopping.

Men did most of the shopping in the agora. We can guess that this market stall is not far from the sea.

Greek merchants traded among the city-states and with other countries around the Mediterranean Sea. Italy sent meat and grain. Scents and spices came from the Middle East. We know that Greek sailors sailed as far as Ireland, Russia, and North Africa. They left behind coins and jewels that could only have come from Greece. Archaeologists have even dived under the sea to look at the wreckage of Greek ships that sank long ago. They can tell from the pots on the seabed that the ships were carrying wine and olive oil.

Vase paintings tell us about people's working lives. On one vase, a shoemaker is cutting a shape in leather around his customer's foot. He will make sure the shoes fit! Some vases show merchants selling olive oil or using scales to weigh out corn. Other vases show women weaving.

The market stalls of the agora have gone, but coins and pieces of pottery have been dug out of the earth. Pottery can be stuck together again, and coins or tools can be cleaned. This is how we know what these things looked like and how they were used.

HISTORY DETECTIVES

The ancient Greeks lived in a land where there was a very long coastline. The sea was part of the people's lives. They needed ships for trade and also to protect themselves from attack from the sea.

The Greeks were excellent shipbuilders. One of the finest warships was the ship in this picture. It was called a trireme because three rows of oarsmen sat on each side of the boat. The ship was easy to steer, and the oarsmen rowed very fast. Experts think that the ship could reach speeds of up to 10 miles (16 kilometers) an hour in calm seas. A trireme also had sails but these and the mast were lowered before a battle.

The bottom of the trireme was made of heavy oak wood, which helped to keep the boat steady. Lighter pine wood was used for the sides of the ship. Even when there were 200 men on board, a trireme could still float in shallow water.

A Greek trireme was about 44 yards (40 meters) long and up to 6.5 yards (6 meters) wide. The front or prow of the boat was made to look like a long sea monster. There was a magic eye painted on the prow that was meant to frighten the enemy. A metal tip on the prow was used to ram other ships. If they did not sink, the trireme would sail close and men would board the other ship to fight.

Triremes were very successful warships. In 480 B.C. the Greeks used these ships to defeat a much bigger Persian fleet. The Greek army had been beaten on land by the Persians, led by King Xerxes. The Persians seized Athens and it looked as if they might take the rest of Greece as well. However, the Greek sailors trapped the Persian ships in a narrow channel, where they attacked and defeated them. Xerxes had to withdraw his troops, and Greece was saved.

The army

Each Greek city-state had its own army. When war came, the citizens had to fight in the army. Sometimes the states fought each other, as happened in 431 B.C. when Athens and the city state of Sparta were at war. At other times the states fought together against foreign enemies.

The Athenian army was led by ten commanders, who were elected by the Assembly. The commanders, or *strategoi*, were each in charge of a regiment of soldiers.

Soldiers who fought on foot were called hoplites. They provided their own weapons and armor. Poorer people, who could not afford a hoplite's armor, were archers and stone slingers. They were called *psiloi*. They wrapped animal skins or cloaks around themselves for protection.

Hoplites fought in a block, or phalanx. There were about eight lines of soldiers in the block. They all moved in step, to the music of a pipe. They charged the enemy until one line broke.

Horse soldiers, or cavalry, were used to break up an enemy phalanx, and were also used as scouts. Each of the ten Athenian tribes had to provide a squadron, or 100 cavalry soldiers. Horse soldiers were armed with spears, javelins, and swords. They wore metal helmets and breastplates.

The Greek hoplite wore leather or metal-plated armor to protect his body and carried a round shield.

When Greek states fought each other, they sometimes surrounded a city with troops. Then they tried to prevent anyone from going in or out of the city. If no food went into the city, they hoped to starve the people into surrender. This was called a siege. They also tried to break down the city walls with battering rams, or to set fire to the city. The Greeks invented a huge catapult to throw large rocks over the walls. They also built siege towers to enable soldiers to climb up onto the city walls. Sometimes there was a catapult in the tower as well as archers.

A Greek soldier saying goodbye to his wife before he goes to war. His shield, sword, helmet, and leg protectors were part of his armor.

Paintings and statues show us what hoplites looked like. Each soldier wore a metal helmet to protect his head and face. The helmet had a piece of horsehair, called a plume, on top. It made the soldiers look taller and more fierce. Clues about soldiers' weapons are given in books by Greek writers, such as the Athenian Xenophon: "Cyrus jumped down from his chariot. He took hold of his spear and told the soldiers to arm themselves too. All wore helmets except Cyrus. All carried swords."

HISTORY DETECTIVES

The painting on this cup shows us what Greek ships looked like. The ship on the right is a trireme, and the ship on the left carried cargo.

15

We do not know a great deal about how Greek homes looked, because few of their buildings have survived. The hot, dry weather meant that the houses were built to keep cool. They usually had one or two levels or floors, and an entrance at the back of the house. Most town homes were made of stone or clay with thatched or tiled roofs. Doors and windows were wooden, and sometimes they had bronze hinges. The buildings were made out of materials that were found nearby.

A Greek house had a number of rooms built around an open courtyard. All the rooms had doors that opened onto the central space. The family ate and sat in the courtyard in good weather. There was usually a table or altar where prayers to Zeus were said, and there might be a well in the courtyard too. Any animals such as pigs, hens, or dogs also lived in the courtyard. Sometimes people cooked there, over an open charcoal fire.

Women and men had special rooms in the house. The women's rooms were called the *gynaeceum*, where they worked and entertained their friends. The men entertained in a room called the *andron*. There were rooms for the slaves, and there was usually a family room with an open fire, which was dedicated to Hestia, the goddess of the hearth. In rich people's houses there would be a bathroom.

The furniture in the house was usually made of wood. In richer homes it might have ivory, silver, or gold decoration. There were tables, stools and chairs, and couches that were used for dining or for sleeping. Clothes were kept in chests of different sizes. At night the rooms were lit by oil lamps. During the day the houses were often dark — since there were few windows — and they were cool. Some rooms had tiled floors, which also helped to keep them cool. In winter, the rooms were heated by burning charcoal in small metal braziers.

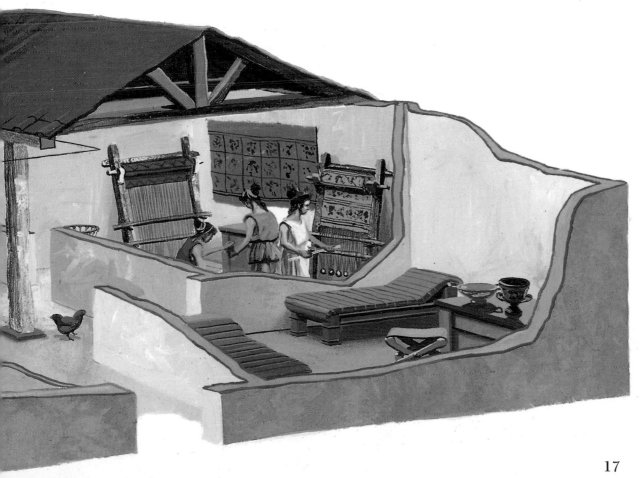

Greek meals

In a Greek home the women or the slaves did the cooking. Meals were prepared in the kitchen, but they were often cooked in the courtyard because of the fire risk. Cooked food was fried in olive oil or stewed in a pan. Breakfast was simply a piece of bread dipped in wine. Then at midday, the hottest time, there was another light meal. This meal might be cheese with a few figs or olives. The main meal was eaten in the late afternoon or evening, and was often a barley porridge and some vegetables.

Men spent little time at home except when friends came to dine. The women of the house brought up the children and taught the girls. Only boys went to school.

Carvings, vase paintings, and toys now in museums show us what children played with. This group of toys (from left to right) includes a whip top, a doll, a baby feeder, a small jug, and a pig-shaped rattle.

Greek meals included salads made from figs, olives, beans, lentils, chick-peas, turnips, leeks, and other vegetables. Olive oil and herbs added to the flavor of the food. Richer people ate more fish and meat. Bread was made from barley flour because wheat was expensive to buy. Bread was often eaten with cheese and local wine. Some people kept bees to provide honey for sweetening food.

At night a rich Greek citizen might hold a banquet. His guests sat or lay on long couches to eat and drink. The women of the house did not usually take part, although sometimes there were other women present. These women were companions, or hetaerae. They were trained to be witty speakers and to play music. The food was served by slaves. As the guests dined, they were entertained by jugglers, acrobats, dancers, or musicians.

Can you find some storage jars like these in the Greek house shown on the previous page? They were called amphorae and were used to store wine and oil.

Greek vase paintings and carvings show scenes from family life. They also show us what furniture looked like. Many pots and storage jars have been dug up, as well as lamps and children's toys. Archaeologists have found the remains of a house in the city of Olynthus, which give us some clues about how an ancient Greek home looked. Many Greek writers have described banquets. These are all evidence about Greek home life.

Boys went to school at the age of seven. They were taught arithmetic and how to read and write on wax tablets. They also learned poetry and how to play the flute. Sports were an important part of school life. Poor families could not afford to send their sons to school.

Greek theater began at a wine festival! Each year, after the grapes had been picked, the wine makers of Greece met to hold a festival. They gave thanks to Dionysus, the god of wine, for the harvest. At these festivals people drank wine, sang, and danced. Some people dressed up in masks and costumes to retell the legends and stories about Dionysus. Telling the stories of Dionysus became a regular event at the festival. In time, the stories turned

into plays. The men who performed at the festival were called the chorus.

Plays were first acted in the marketplace. In Athens, the people built a stone theater inside the curve of a hill. It was on the Acropolis, near the temple of Dionysus. The seats on the slopes looked down over the stage below.

Later, theaters were built in many other places, as plays became very popular. Important people, or judges at drama competitions, sat at the front.

The plays

In the first plays, the chorus of men danced and sang in a large circle that was about 22 yards (20 meters) wide. The circle was called the orchestra, which means place in which to dance. An altar to Dionysus stood in the middle of the orchestra. From this simple start, the Greeks went on to write and perform some of the finest plays ever written. They built huge theaters that seated thousands of people. The theater at Epidaurus, for instance, had 55 rows of seats, one above the other. It could seat 16,000 people, which is five to ten times as many as most theaters today.

Euripedes, Aeschylus, and Sophocles were three of the leading Greek writers, or playwrights. They wrote about heroines and heroes from Greek history, and about gods and goddesses. Often their plays were very sad. These plays were called tragedies. Aristophanes wrote funny plays about ordinary people. They were called comedies. Many of the words we use to describe theaters and plays come from Greek words. They include words such as "tragedy," "comedy," and "scenery."

Only male actors acted in a Greek play. They wore masks to show the sort of part they were playing. A smiling mask showed a happy person. Other masks depicted angry or evil people. The puffed-out shape of the mask made the actor's voice louder and easier to hear in the huge open-air theater.

22

Performances in the Greek theater often lasted all day. Most people paid to go in, but very poor people did not pay. Huge crowds began to stand in line at dawn in order to get a good seat.

At each performance there were usually three long tragedies and then a shorter play that made people laugh. The actors changed into their costumes in a hut at the back of the stage. They called the hut a *skene*. Pictures were painted on the front of the *skene* to hide it from the audience. These pictures later became the scenery in a play. The Greeks also used special effects in their plays. Real chariots and horses made the plays more exciting, and stones rattling in a bronze bowl sounded like thunder. Simple cranes and thin ropes were used to make the actors who played gods fly through the air.

In the Greek theater actors wore padded costumes and wigs. Tragic actors wore black costumes. Happy characters wore bright colors and patterned costumes.

Many of the Greek plays, such as *The Wasps* by Aristophanes and *King Oedipus* by Sophocles, are still performed today. They are often staged in the open air in the ruined theaters of ancient Greece where they were first performed over 2,000 years ago.

HISTORY DETECTIVES

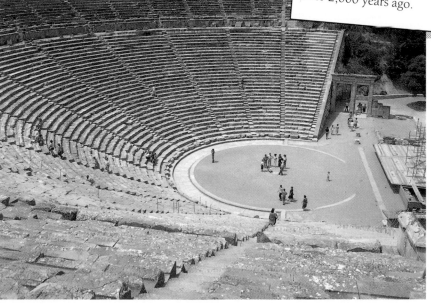

Visitors to Epidaurus can see for themselves how well the Greeks built their theaters. Its stone seats still stand on the terraces, which were cut into the hillside. Everyone had a good view of the orchestra below. Even today, everyone in the theater can hear an actor speaking without a microphone.

23

The Greeks encouraged people to keep fit. They thought that exercise made people healthy. This was important in times of war, when soldiers had to be fit to fight. Young men in all the city-states competed in athletic contests. The most famous of these contests was held every four years at Olympia. The Olympic Games were so important that wars between states were halted to allow the soldiers to compete and to make sure that people could travel safely to attend. The Games were held to honor Zeus, whose special flame burned in the sacred olive grove at Olympia.

The first Olympic Games were held in 776 B.C. and every four years afterward for a thousand years. They took place in June or July and lasted for five days. Since this was a sacred event, the huge crowds that flocked to Olympia were more like pilgrims than sports fans. Everyone brought a gift for Zeus or for one of the other gods.

All the fields near the stadium at Olympia were full of tents and people sleeping in the open air, because there were no hotels or places for the visitors to stay. Traders sold food and other goods from market stalls. They made the event more like a country fair than a religious or sporting occasion.

The events

At the Games the young men took part in many of the events which are still held today at the Olympic Games. They ran races over long and short distances. Some threw the javelin or the discus. Others took part in boxing or wrestling contests. Each athlete had to obey a set of rules. Slaves could not take part in the Games, and women were not even allowed to watch. Women had their own Games, which were also held every four years. They were called the Hereia, in honour of the goddess Hera.

There were other Greek sports as well as athletics. Ball games were popular. Vase paintings and carvings show games which look very like the modern games of hockey and football.

The Olympic Games began at dawn with a trumpet call. The list of men who were taking part was read out, and they had to swear before the gods that they would not cheat, and that they had trained properly for the Games. Each race also started with a trumpet call. The winners were crowned with olive branches.

Chariot racing was another popular Olympic sport. The chariots were drawn by teams of two or four horses. They raced at high speed in the hippodrome.

Some athletes took part in the pentathlon. They had to perform five tasks one after the other. They had to wrestle, run, long jump, throw the discus, and throw the javelin. The Greeks took pride in being good at many things. This is why poets, dancers, and musicians, as well as athletes, went to the Olympic Games to compete for prizes. The Games were not simply an athletic contest.

About one hundred years ago, archaeologists found evidence about the Olympic Games. They discovered the temple to Zeus, the sacred olive grove, the stadium where the races were run, and the horse track, or hippodrome, where the riding and chariot races were held.

We even know how the races were run, because the stone starting line was found at Olympia. It is marked out by stone slabs which are each about 2 feet (half a meter) wide. Vase paintings show runners in one race wearing armor and carrying a shield. This would have been good training for soldiers. There are many other pictures of athletic contests.

HISTORY DETECTIVES

Greek sports were tests of skill. Competitors had to be fit and strong to throw the discus like this.

The discus thrower tested his skill by throwing a flat, round stone or disk that weighed about 14 or 15 pounds (6 or 7 kilograms).

In 1896 a Frenchman, Baron Pierre de Coubertin, organized the first modern Olympic Games. They are based on the Games of ancient Greece, and a flame is lit to start the competition. They are still held every four years, and men and women from all over the world now take part.

B.C.	(before the birth of Christ)
c. 850	Birth of the poet, Homer
776	First Olympic Games
700	Athens joins with nearby towns and villages to form a city-state
c. 600	Birth of the poetess, Sappho
594	Solon elected as *archon* — the leader of Athens
c. 580	Birth of the mathematician, Pythagoras
561	A tyrant named Peisistratus seizes power in Athens
c. 550	Anaximander draws a map of the world
c. 525	Birth of the playwright, Aeschylus
c. 522	Birth of the poet, Pindar
507	Athens becomes a democracy once again
c. 495	Birth of the playwright, Sophocles
490	The Greeks defeat Darius of Persia at the Battle of Marathon
c. 490	Birth of the sculptor, Phidias
c. 490	Birth of Pericles
480	A Persian army defeats the Greeks at Thermopylae but its navy is defeated soon afterward by a Greek fleet at Salamis
c. 480	Birth of the playwright, Euripides
479	Greeks defeat Persians at the Battle of Plataea
c. 470	Birth of the philosopher, Socrates
464	Rebellion by slaves in Sparta
462	Pericles persuades the Athenians to accept a number of reforms
c. 460	Birth of the physician, Hippocrates
456	Death of the playwright, Aeschylus
c. 450	Birth of the playwright, Aristophanes
447	Building of the Parthenon begins

438	Parthenon finished
431	War between Athens and Sparta
430	Plague kills many people in Athens
429	Death of Pericles
427	Birth of the philosopher, Plato
c. 424	Death of the historian, Herodotus
412	Birth of the philosopher, Diogenes
408	Completion of the Erechtheum on the Acropolis in Athens
406	Death of the playwrights Sophocles and Euripides
405	Spartan fleet commanded by Lysander defeats the Athenian triremes at the Battle of Aegosapotami
404	Defeat of Athens by Sparta
399	Socrates ends his life by taking poison
385	Plato opens a school for philosophers in Athens
384	Birth of the philosopher, Aristotle
359	Philip II becomes ruler of Macedonia
338	Philip II of Macedonia defeats the Athenians and becomes ruler of Greece
336	Philip II assassinated. He is succeeded by his young son Alexander
335	Alexander the Great makes sure the Greeks are loyal to his regime
334	Alexander the Great begins his conquest of the Persian Empire by defeating a Persian army at the Battle of Granicus
333	Alexander the Great defeats the Persians at the Battle of Issus
331	Alexander finally controls the Persian Empire after defeating Darius III at the Battle of Arbela
325	Alexander the Great completes his conquest of an empire stretching from Athens in the west to the Indus valley (now in Pakistan) in the east
323	Alexander the Great dies of fever at the age of 32

Aeschylus: a leading Greek playwright, known for his tragedies

agora: the square and marketplace in the center of a Greek city

altar: a stone or wooden table where prayers were said and sacrifices were made to the gods and goddesses

andron: the room where men entertained in a house

archaeologist: a scientist who studies the past through the relics and ruins left behind by people in the past

Aristophanes: a leading Greek playwright, known for his comedies

Assembly: the name given to the meeting that all male adult citizens of Athens attended in order to discuss and vote on matters that affected them all

Athena: the daughter of Zeus and goddess of wisdom and skills. She also protected many Greek cities, such as Athens.

Athens: the most important city in ancient Greece

cargo: goods carried by ship

catapult: a wooden weapon that fired rocks and was used in siege warfare

cavalry: soldiers who fought on horseback

charcoal: a fuel made by roasting wood slowly

city-state: a city and surrounding area that governed itself

comedy: a play that is lighthearted and makes you laugh

democracy: a system in which every person has some say in how a country is governed

Dionysus: the Greek god of wine

Epidaurus: A Greek town that was famous for its huge theater

Erechtheum: a large temple built on the Acropolis in Athens

Euripides: a leading Greek playwright who wrote tragedies

Greek chorus: the group of male singers who sang and danced in Greek plays

gynaeceum: the women's rooms in a house

hetaerae: women who were trained to entertain. They were amusing speakers and talented musicians.

hippodrome: a Greek stadium where chariot races were held. "*Hippos*" was the Greek word for horse.

Homer: a famous Greek writer who is thought to have lived about 2,800 years ago

hoplite: a Greek soldier who wore armor and fought on foot

mint: a government building where coins are made

Mount Olympus: a mountain in northern Greece. The Greeks believed it was the home of Zeus and all the gods and goddesses.

olive: the black fruit of the olive tree, which grows only in hot countries such as Greece and Italy. It is used to make olive oil.

Olympia: the place in southern Greece where the first Olympic Games were held in 776 B.C.

orchestra: the 22 yard (20 meter) wide circle in which the Greek *chorus* sang and danced

Parthenon: the great temple to Athena at the top of the Acropolis

phalanx: a block of soldiers who moved together in battle

playwright: a writer of plays

plume: the feathers on a soldier's helmet

podium: a raised step on which a speaker can stand in order to be seen and heard by a crowd

Poseidon: the Greek god of the sea

Propylaea: the huge gateway to the Acropolis

prow: the front of a boat

psiloi: poor men who fought as foot soldiers. They had no armor.

skene: the hut in a Greek theater where the actors changed. It was later painted over to become part of the scenery used in the play.

siege: an attempt to starve a town or city into surrender

siege tower: a wooden tower. It was moved up close to a city wall. The soldiers inside it could attack soldiers on the walls and also climb onto the walls.

Sophocles: a leading Greek playwright who wrote tragedies

Sparta: a powerful Greek city and a rival of Athens

squadron: a group of 100 cavalry soldiers

story: a floor or level in a building

strategoi: leaders of the armed forces. They helped to plan how the wars were fought

theater mask: a mask used by male Greek actors to enable them to play different parts

tragedy: a play with a serious story and often an unhappy ending

trireme: a powerful Greek warship pulled through the water by 200 oarsmen

vase painting: a picture painted on the sides of a pot or vase

Xerxes: a king of Persia

Zeus: the king of the gods

For Further Reading

Adams, Jean-Pierre. *Mediterranean Civilizations*. Needham Heights, Massachusetts: Silver, Burdett & Ginn, 1987.

Cohen, Daniel. *Ancient Greece*. New York: Doubleday, 1990.

Evslin, Bernard. *Greek Gods*. New York: Scholastic, 1988.

Miquel, Pierre. *Life in Ancient Greece*. Needham Heights, Massachusetts: Silver Burdett & Ginn, 1986.

Powell, Anton. *The Greek World*. New York: Warwick, 1987.

Ross, Harriet, ed. *Greek Myths: Tales of the Gods, Heroes and Heroines*. Scarsdale, New York: Lion Books, 1988.

Rutland, Jonathan. *Ancient Greek Town*, rev. ed. New York: Warwick, 1986.

Switzer, Ellen. *Greek Myths: Gods, Heroes and Monsters — Their Sources, Their Stories and Their Meanings*. New York: Atheneum, 1988.